Most Schools Won't Fit

SECOND EDITION

The Epidemic of
Disengagement
and
What To Do
About It

Don Berg and Holly Allen

Attitutor

2nd Edition, 2023

1st Edition, 2017

Attitutor LLC., West Linn, Oregon 97068

For more information, visit HolisticEquity.org

ISBN: 978-0-9994888-8-1 (paperback)

ISBN: 978-0-9994888-9-8 (epub)

Contents

It ain't what you don't know that gets you into trouble. It's what you know for sure that just ain't so.

~ Anonymous, but often misattributed to Mark Twain or other comedians of the 1870's

Much of what is called educational "reform" does not work. It fails because it is based on false assumptions. What is scary is that these false assumptions arise naturally. The assumptions may seem right at first glance. But they are false, and they are harmful. You don't see bacteria and viruses, but they can harm you and your kids. Similarly, you may not be aware of the unconscious ideas you've inherited, but they are there and they can be disastrous.

~ From George Lakoff's foreward to Dumb Ideas Won't Create Smart Kids by Eric Haas, Gustavo Fischman, & Joe Brewer

Chapter One

The Epidemic of Disengagement

This is the story of how our school system, under the influence of a wrong idea, harms its participants. Despite the fact that experts in at least two fields — psychology and education — overwhelmingly recognize the idea as false, its influence has steadily grown in the last fifty years. Intuitively compelling and simple to implement, it guides educational policy in ways that sound reasonable on paper but utterly fail in practice.

The idea is about how people learn, which we call the delivery model. The famous education activist and scholar Paulo Freire called it the banking model. Other scholars and commentators have different names for it. The core concept is that one person can take knowledge out of his own brain and stuff it into someone else's.

My co-author, Holly Allen, and I approach the delivery method from different perspectives. I have come to understand the delivery model and its effects after more than two decades of working with children in self-directed educational systems and studying psychology. I am one of only a few researchers who have studied the motivational patterns of students in non-mainstream settings.

For Allen, the importance of the delivery model is immediate and personal: She has three young children. Drawing on her own educational experiences, degrees in biochemistry and computer science, and her experience as a parent, she's been searching for how best to help her children succeed in the world without running afoul of the downsides of mainstream education.

A Historical Perspective

At no time in history have we better understood how our own minds work or how learning occurs, yet almost none of that understanding has influenced our educational system, public or private.

This is, on the face of it, a fantastic claim. We tend to assume that greater understanding leads almost automatically to better systems. Once we figured out how to build houses, it no longer made sense to live in caves.

Once we figured out that germs cause contagious diseases, it no longer made sense to bleed people to "balance their humors" (and too often kill them,[1] as happened to George Washington). Once we figured out how to build electronic computers, it no longer made sense to employ armies of people to make manual calculations.[2]

Anyone with even a little knowledge of schooling over the past century might also be forgiven for being skeptical of such a claim. After all, haven't there been countless waves of reform in that time — new methods of teaching math, reading, spelling, and history? What about open classrooms, project-based learning, and jigsaw classrooms? What about recent technological innovations, such as

---

1. The switch from the miasma theory, which called for "balancing humors," to the germ theory is described in both Steven Johnson's 2006 book, The Ghost Map, and in medical historian David Wootton's 2007 book, Bad Medicine.

2. The based on a true story and Academy Award-nominated movie, Hidden Figures, tells the tale of how the term computers at NASA changed its reference point from women to electronic equipment during the sixties space race.

electronic whiteboards and the One Laptop-per-Child initiative?

But all the reforms and innovations that have been so ardently pursued in schools have been about as meaningful as nineteenth-century physicians arguing over which particular vein to pierce and how much blood to let flow.

Here's why.

The Familiar Problem

First, let's revisit the problem. Chances are that if you're reading this, you're aware that the American school system is considered to be in a crisis that threatens to destroy our national prosperity and way of life. Our test scores — the measurements on which our society depends more and more heavily as an indicator of success — remain consistently mediocre despite ever more desperate reforms. Of more immediate impact is that the students who graduate from our high schools are routinely found to be ill prepared for either college or the workforce, and employers are no more enthusiastic about those graduating from college.[3] Even if we simply want to

---

3. Berr (2016)

prepare people for the workforce, we are not doing a very good job.

If you have higher aspirations for education — for example, that it might help people fulfill their own potential, learn to think well, or become good citizens — you are likely to be even more disappointed.

This problem is not new. In the last two centuries, school has become a nearly universal part of childhood throughout the world. Today, children in this country spend more than half of their waking hours in school. We have a deeply vested interest in anything that impacts our children, and with the weight on school to provide our kids with all the skills and knowledge they need to prosper in the world, it's no wonder we focus so much attention on it. For years, decades — arguably centuries — people have been talking about how to fix the school system.

Most of the proposed fixes, even those proposed a century ago, sound familiar. New methods of presenting material are always popular and always hotly contested. (Try livening up the conversation among a group of parents by throwing out the phrase "whole language versus phonics.") As testing has become more influential, proposals to test more often and more rigorously have gained support. Push people harder, and they'll perform better, right?

At the same time, interestingly, material is often simplified to remove any nuance or ambiguity that might cause a child to stumble. And money is always a heated topic. Even adjusted for inflation, we spend more than twice as much per student now as we did fifty years ago.[4] In fact, we (in the USA) spend more per student than most countries in the world, including those that consistently score higher than we do on standardized tests.

Then there's the push for teacher accountability. The teachers are the ones who are supposed to be doing the actual work in these crucial school settings; they're responsible for making certain that each child reaches his or her potential. So why not focus on measuring and incentivizing teacher effectiveness, so we can reward good teachers and weed out the bad ones?

Looking back on even just the recent decades of school reform, surveying the dizzying array of programs aimed at improving education, it's easy to feel a bit overwhelmed — "No Child Left Behind," "Race to the Top," and the "Every Student Succeeds Act" are the names of just the central federal programs since 2001. And inevitably, if one can step back from the morass for a few minutes, another question arises: Why hasn't any of this worked?

---

4. U.S. Department of Education (2005)

Or, when we do declare a reform successful, why are the improvements so small?

Despite all the ideas and work and restructuring, things aren't improving. In some ways, things seem to be getting worse. The usual culprits are lined up: We aren't using the right methods of teaching, we don't offer students the right incentives to perform, we don't invest enough money in our educational system, and we can't get rid of the "bad" teachers.

But the truth is that all these reforms are working around the edges of the central issue, one that goes unrecognized by the majority of parents, media, and policymakers. There is a fundamental problem in our approach to education, a problem that undermines all the good intentions of the many talented and passionate people involved.

And we can begin to grasp the problem by considering its most direct and pervasive symptom: disengagement.

Widespread Disengagement

Disengagement gets an occasional mention in discussions about school, but only as a side issue. Students typically start school with all the excitement that characterizes being six years old, and somewhere along the way their enthusiasm fades. And this isn't just an informal observation. For more than thirty years, researchers have studied patterns of motivation in mainstream schools repeatedly. Using a variety of theoretical and methodological approaches, all studies of mainstream schools — public, private, and charter — have documented the same effect: Statistically, student engagement declines throughout the entire span of compulsory schooling.[5] The phenomenon is so widespread that many people accept it as inevitable.

What does disengagement look like? In students, there are three main symptoms:

1. Some students simply drop out. This is the simplest and most obvious form of disengagement. Dropping out is usually preceded by the student tuning out, often years earlier.

2. Some students remain in school but fail to

---

5. References regarding declines in engagement and intrinsic motivation: Bouffard, Marcoux, Vezeau, & Bordeleau (2003), Corpus, McClintic-Gilbert, & Hayenga (2009), Gottfried, Fleming, & Gottfried (2001), Harter (1981), Hunter, & Csikszentmihalyi (2003), Lepper, Corpus, & Iyengar (2005)

perform. Underachievement can have a variety of faces — there seems to be a vast difference between a student who consistently tries, yet struggles, and one who rejects his or her schooling — but the net effect is similar.

3. This third, less recognized symptom is fauxchievement. Fauxchievement is when a student does the required work to achieve whatever minimal grade he or she finds acceptable but fails to actually engage with the material. The student is playing the game, jumping through the hoops, but emotionally he or she has checked out.

This last symptom may seem harmless — in fact, doesn't everyone do that? But there's a long-term consequence to faking one's way through school. Studies on adults found that at least half of all college degree holders managed to get their degrees without fundamentally understanding basic principles.[6] This means that they are unable to solve the most basic problems in their field of specialization when those problems are presented in a real-world manner. In

---

6. Gardner (2004)

other words, they've jumped through all the right hoops but have failed to really master the concepts.

Think about that. How would you feel knowing that your brain surgeon failed to grasp basic medical concepts? The evidence cited earlier implies that this is actually true of at least half of all doctors.

And the epidemic of disengagement isn't limited to students. Adults are also infected. Even teachers report disengagement at the same levels as the overall US workforce — about 70%. Despite the huge number of passionate, idealistic teachers entering the field each year, nearly a fifth fail to last even five years. Of those who remain, almost three-quarters are disengaged from their work — the work of molding our children.

You might wonder why we believe that disengagement is more important to talk about than funding, equity, or any of the other topics that dominate media coverage of education. Exploring the causes of disengagement gets at a root issue, one that must be addressed in order for any other improvements to have sustainable impacts. This is not to claim that other issues are unimportant, only that addressing disengagement is a necessary foundation for creating meaningful improvements that will not be undermined by the next change in the political winds.

It's no coincidence that both students and teachers are impacted by the epidemic of disengagement. At heart, both teaching and learning are inherently creative endeavors, and they're both susceptible to the same psychological pitfalls. Moreover, there's evidence that engagement is contagious — and so is disengagement. An engaged teacher is more likely to stimulate engagement in his or her students, and engaged students help a teacher maintain his or her own engagement. Unfortunately, the same is true of disengagement.

Right now, disengagement is in the lead. If we want schools that provide a better educational experience, we need to understand why so many of the people involved in the learning process fall prey to some form of disengagement. We can gain some understanding by observing engaged students and teachers. It's worth considering school environments where the inevitability of disengagement does not exist and engagement is the norm. This turns out to be a difficult challenge since it requires us to get out of the mainstream, which serves well over 90% of all students. It is only since 2009 that we have scientifically credible evidence that a different pattern is even possible.

Chapter Two

Immunity From Disengagement

There are schools that keep both students and teachers engaged, and if we're interested in truly effective education, it's worth investigating how they do that.

Consider the following two schools, both based in or near Portland, Oregon. The first is the Village Home Education Resource Center, which provides classes to homeschooling families, operating like a community college for students in pre-kindergarten through high school. Village Home is aimed at family-directed education; in other words, it provides classes and resources, but expects families to be actively engaged in managing the education of their children. Students can choose to take as many or as few classes as they like, and age restrictions are broad and flexible, with students encouraged to take classes based on their interests and abilities. Classes run the gamut, from highly structured classes in math, science, and literature, to a variety of more unusual and less academic courses, such as embroidery and wilderness skills. Some classes are taught by parents, but most are taught by professional teachers who have often come from the public education system.

Village Home uses no grading and no standardized curriculum in order to avoid competition and comparison among students. Each class identifies up front whether homework is required, optional, or nonexistent, and students can further choose the level of intensity of a teacher's feedback. For example, if a student wants a teacher to rigorously evaluate an essay, with every misspelling or missing comma noted, they will specifically ask for "hard" feedback.

In contrast, the similarly named but completely unrelated Village Free School (VFS) is a democratic school, where everyone — from the youngest student to the most senior member of the staff — has an identical vote in the running of the school (with certain legal and safety issues aside). Three foundational rules have been in place since the school was founded: Take care of yourself and other people, take care of the things the school and other people own, and remember that your freedom ends where someone else's begins.

Students divide roughly into three groups based on age and inclination, but the boundaries between those groups are porous, and students spend much of their time interacting in mixed-age groups. Classes (or "offerings" in VFS terminology) can be created by any staff or student, are often collaborations, and are always optional. Classes for the oldest students may follow a formal class model, but those for younger students rarely do. Daily rhythms are established by the community and can be voted out or changed at any time.

The school day has evolved significantly since VFS's inception in 2004, and it continues to change. In 2017, the youngest group of students engaged mostly in free play, although the children were welcome to join in on offerings and field trips as they liked. The middle group of students adhered to mornings spent in "Project Time." Project Time was a student invention where every kid was required to be working on something — the specific project they chose was up to them — and adults were available to assist them. The oldest group has experimented with a variety of formats over the years, and they put together a more defined curriculum of life skills and academic classes.

You might imagine that neither of these schools could prepare young people for the real world. Yet many graduates from both schools have gone on to college and done very well in that setting. Other graduates have plunged straight into working in fields they found interesting and challenging. Most important for our discussion is the fact that these two schools are based on very different models of education, yet share an interesting common trait: In both schools, disengagement is almost unheard of.[1]

The epidemic of disengagement is nearly ubiquitous in the mainstream education system, regardless of whether schools are public, private, or charter. How do Village Home and VFS manage to avoid this epidemic?

To answer this question, I offer an analogy. Let's take a brief detour to London more than a century ago.

The Wrong Paradigm

Mainstream education today is in the same position as medicine in the mid-1800s: It's based on the wrong model. London in the mid-1800s had been growing at an exponential rate for decades to become the most

---

1. Berg & Corpus (2013)

populated city in the world with over 2 million people. The place was packed with both humans and the animals they kept: horses to get around, cows and pigs for food, pets, etc. Remember that everyone and their animals all poop. The most common places to dump the poop, when they didn't just throw it in the street, was in cesspools that were dug into vacant lots nearby or in their basements. The place was permeated by an unavoidable stench. They called those bad smells miasma.

Most people in the world in the 1800s believed that the miasma caused epidemic diseases, like cholera. Ridicule and scorn met those who were bold enough to assert that the cause of cholera could be invisible particles in the water, a hypothesis that was later proven to be true.

In 1848, London passed the "Nuisances Removal and Contagious Disease Prevention Act," legislation aimed at getting rid of the noxious materials (including large amounts of raw human sewage) fouling London's streets. The act authorized a large-scale project, which would get that waste out of sight and out of mind, sending it into the stormwater system, an underground system of pipes. Those pipes eventually dumped their contents into the river Thames, which lay at the heart of the city and provided, among other things, the drinking water for two-thirds of the city's residents.

In 1854, the worst outbreak of cholera ever in the world, before or since, occurred in London. Dr. John Snow was one of the ridiculed champions of the unpopular idea that we now call germ theory. After the outbreak started, Snow visited one neighborhood where it was raging and met a local clergyman named Henry Whitehead. Whitehead believed in the miasma theory of disease but agreed to help Snow in order to prove him wrong.

Together they collected enough clear and compelling evidence to prove to Whitehead, and many others, that the disease could not possibly have been spread through the air. The mass death in the Reverend Whitehead's neighborhood was caused by something in the water, specifically from the Broad Street pump.

Patient zero was an infant. But the true origin of that outbreak was a soiled diaper. It was thrown into a leaky basement cesspool that contaminated the water in the Broad Street well, which was ironically reputed to have the best water in the city.

During the implementation of the act from 1848 the authorities missed the cesspool where patient zero's infected diaper ended up, probably because it was hidden away in a basement. But, even if it had, that might have made things worse, not better. Those stormwater pipes eventually dumped their contents into the river Thames, which was a major source of drinking water at the heart of the city.

Now, remember that the Water Board thought that it was the smells that caused disease. The members of the Water Board felt the urgency of the issue and inadvertently created a worse problem by ensuring that germ-laden sewage would contaminate the drinking water for most of the city's residents. Also remember that for about six years they felt very good about how much of the stink they were eliminating. Their removal of the nuisance smells was obviously successful, but they did not realize that their strategy for preventing disease made that problem worse.

Any modern person, raised with the concept of germ theory, knows that dumping raw sewage into drinking water supplies is a terrible idea. Under the miasma model, getting all that filth off the streets was vitally important; where it went was irrelevant. The 1848 legislation can be viewed as a large-scale endorsement of miasma theory. After a great deal of work and a huge public investment, London's streets were much cleaner and the city's smell improved. But epidemics of cholera subsequently killed tens of thousands more people, many of those deaths being a result of mixing sewage with drinking water.[2]

Miasma theory was not just a single idea. It was the central defining feature of a whole suite of concepts that provided explanations for both health and disease. Those concepts in turn led to a variety of medical treatments, such as bloodletting and purging (inducing vomiting, sweating, and evacuation of the bowels) that were widely used to treat disease. Miasma theory is intuitively logical — after all, having bad-smelling things like feces and carrion around did often correlate with disease, and some people who received the common treatments got better. It also had generations of tradition behind it. For experts and lay people alike, it was a paradigm that shaped everyday thinking about health and disease for centuries.

And it was quite simply wrong.

Education today is in a state similar to that of medicine when the Thames delivered death to London's residents.

---

2. This is not to imply that cholera would have been otherwise absent; Steven Berlin Johnson reports in his 2006 book The Ghost Map that given the death tolls before and after the legislated project's completion, it is reasonable to conclude that tens of thousands more people died than might have done had germ theory guided policy decisions.

The dominant paradigm driving educational legislation today is the delivery model, and it remains firmly rooted in our educational policies despite the impressive quantity and variety of research undermining it. *Simply put, the delivery model considers the core of education to be delivering information from a teacher's head into a student's head.* How well that task has been accomplished is measured by testing the students afterward.

Howard Gardner, Professor of Cognition and Education at the Harvard Graduate School of Education, summed it up this way: "You go to school, a smart person tells you something, and you are expected to learn it and remember it, and if you don't, you are stupid." He went on to say that "...rarely is there any conception of learning as a long process of (children's) experimentation, reflection, and self-improvement." He also noted that many people continue to entertain the mistaken delivery notion even after reaching adulthood.[3]

Policymakers working under the delivery model quite logically reason that accounting for information delivery is what really matters in education. It makes sense to standardize all the information and break it down into small chunks, so that as each chunk is delivered, it can

---

3. Gardner (2004) p. 102.

be checked off the list, like a FedEx driver marking off his packages. Teachers, who are the active elements in this model, are "graded" based on how effective their package delivery was (i.e., how much content is now in each student's head). The very concept of "teacher-proof curricula" inherently assumes that teachers just need to deliver the content correctly for optimal learning to happen.

The intuitive logic of the delivery model is compelling — after all, students must be exposed to information in order to learn it — and has resulted in what seems to be complete political consensus that improving schools requires only standardized tests and standardized curricula. Hundreds of billions of dollars in public investment in the United States have endorsed this theory of education in the form of both state and federal laws that mandate standardized testing and make funding contingent on checking off all the right boxes.

According to renowned global-education scholar Yong Zhao,[4] the Chinese mastered this idea thousands of years ago, with horrible long-term consequences for their nation. Now they are doing everything they can to get their systems away from the curses of high-stakes testing

4. Zhao (2009)

and universal standardization. Because they do not have a viable replacement paradigm for learning, the Chinese have been struggling with little success for over a decade to bring about meaningful change. They are in a mighty fight against what is for most people the obvious truth about learning.

In fact, although you may not have heard it described in such straightforward terms, the delivery model may seem reasonable to you. It may even sound like common sense. You may, depending on your own experiences, have the uneasy feeling that perhaps it isn't the whole story. If you're a parent, for example, you may have noticed that young children don't seem to work this way. If you're a teacher, you probably know it isn't remotely correct, but more on that later. Once out of school, you may have even noticed that you don't work this way. But generations of Americans (and Chinese) have gone through the public education system and have learned that this is how things work. Teachers impart knowledge, students parrot it back, and that, in a nutshell, is learning.

Unfortunately, this delivery model is wrong. And like miasma theory, policies based on it are doing more harm than good. In particular, this delivery model encourages policies that directly work against some of our primary human needs.

What Are Primary Human Needs?

There are certain things every human needs in order to function well. We need air, food, and water; we need shelter from the elements; and we need sleep. These five examples are commonly understood, and the school system generally recognizes their impact on learning. Subsidized lunch programs attempt to make certain that every student has enough to eat, for example. And kids and their parents are urged to make sure the kids are getting enough sleep, so they can be ready for their day.

But there are three other primary human needs that are well understood in psychological circles but are only beginning to drift into general public awareness: autonomy, competence, and relatedness. In this book, we refer to supporting another person's primary human needs as nurturing — not in a general warm and fuzzy way, but as a psychologically specific term.

Autonomy is exactly what it sounds like: feeling that we engage in activities of our own volition. In Western societies, this is nearly always associated with making choices for ourselves, but it's worth noting that if two people share a strong enough connection (for example, a strong bond of trust between a parent and a child), directions from the person in authority can still support autonomy under the right conditions. None of us, of course, have complete control over our lives; we all abide by rules from a wide variety of sources, ranging from our legal system to social norms. But all of us know the difference between being helpless and feeling that we have some power to affect our lives.

Competence refers to the sense of mastery we experience as we improve our skills. We perform best when we take on tasks that are within our abilities but that still stretch us slightly. If tasks are too hard, we tend to be frustrated; too easy, and we get bored.[5]

Finally, relatedness is our need to feel connected to other people and to feel that they recognize us for who we are. This is not as simple as having people be nice to us; we must feel that we are seen and respected for our authentic selves.

---

5. Educators might associate this description with Lev Vygotsky's zone of proximal development and psychologists with Mihaly Csikzentmihalyi's flow state. Those associations are sensible though in technical terms they are all three somewhat different from each other because of how the ideas were developed from different theoretical and research traditions.

It's tempting to put these into a category other than "needs." We sometimes use phrases that suggest that autonomy, for example, is more of a nice-to-have quality. The phrase "beggars can't be choosers" implies that choice is more of a luxury and, perhaps, something that we must earn. But cognitive psychological research has overwhelmingly demonstrated the importance of all primary human needs. Being deprived of autonomy may not kill you, but all humans react to the loss of any of these primary human needs with anxiety, depression, and other forms of psychological distress. They may also resort to increasingly desperate and, perhaps, even anti-social attempts to reestablish it.

The tie-in to psychological disorders like depression is particularly worrying. Boston College developmental psychologist Peter Gray has recently written about the research of Jean Twenge that reveals the declining mental health of American school children going back to the 1940s, when properly validated measures of these phenomena were first used.[6] The steady increases in anxiety and depression don't seem to correlate with external threats (e.g., the economic recession or the Cold War). Instead, increasing depression correlates

---

6. Gray (2013)

closely with the increase in children's time spent in highly structured, externally-imposed activities (including ever greater amounts of school) and the corresponding decrease in free play. In fact, in 2014, suicide was the second most common cause of death among middle-school-aged children in the United States.

The Dilemma

Parents are on the horns of the following dilemma: Their parental responsibility in today's world is to find a school that supports the well-being of their children, so they can live a normal adult life while their kids learn how to grow up to be awesome people. But mainstream schools — the primary institutions that are responsible for supplying and organizing child-nurturing people — have a system in place that actively interferes with the ability of the people in schools to do that job.

- Dropouts are alienated from school instead of welcomed into it, so they disengage from it. Their primary human need for relatedness has been thwarted. According to a 2016 report issued by the National Center for Education Statistics,[7]

---

7. NCES (2016)

the risk of dropout was lowest for white kids (at one in twenty-two) and highest for Latinx kids (at about one in eleven), with all other racial groups falling somewhere in between for an overall average of about one in seventeen.

- Underachievers experience schools as controlling places where they do not have adequate self-expression, so they disengage from the majority of classroom activities. Their primary human need for autonomy has been thwarted. According to the 2009 High School Transcript Study,[8] also from the National Center for Education Statistics, one in four graduates are below curriculum standards.

- Fauxchievers experience schools as arbitrary systems to be gamed. So while their behavior might suggest they are engaged in school, they are agentically disengaged from some or all of their subjects and do an absolute minimum of work to get whatever level of scores or grades they deem necessary. Their primary human need

---

8. Nord, et al. (2011)

for competence has been thwarted. According to Howard Gardner in his 2004 book *The Unschooled Mind*, at least one in two of those who go on to advanced degrees in their field do so by fauxchievement.

No matter how you slice it, there is a significant risk that the school system will cheat your child out of some or all of the education he or she deserves. Children can be cheated in several ways, but the odds of being cheated are good if you stick to typical mainstream schools, regardless of whether the schools they attend are public, private, or charter. And marginalized populations run the highest risks. Economics, tradition, and widespread community support encourage parents to choose mainstream schools. However, when parents are made aware of the risks involved with attending mainstream schools, their instinctive capacity for nurturing might lead them in the opposite direction.

Getting an education today in mainstream schools is comparable to surviving disease up until the early twentieth century: You might manage it, but it will be in spite of the dominant paradigm, not because of it. The core idea of delivery that guides educational policy today makes it more and more likely that harms will be delivered more reliably than benefits.

To be clear, this isn't a recent problem. According to Eric Haas, Gustavo Fischman, and Joe Brewer in their 2014 book *Dumb Ideas Won't Create Smart Kids*, there is evidence that the ideas that have informed the design of schools have been fundamentally the same for at least four thousand years. Different cultures at different times have implemented them in a variety of ways, but the core theories have been consistently wrong.

What's changed in recent history (i.e., the last hundred years or more) is the scale on which the delivery model has been implemented. After all, poor sanitation was always a problem for London — but societal changes in the eighteenth and nineteenth centuries began to make it a truly urgent issue. Cholera only started killing Londoners en masse in the early 1800s after population density rose dramatically. Similarly, the delivery model has always been wrong, but as long as schools were relatively small and locally controlled, there was opportunity for people to instinctively lessen their ill effects. But as external pressure has mounted on schools — to increasingly centralize school management since the forties, to focus on science and math since the beginning of the Cold War in the late fifties and early sixties, to increasingly standardize all subjects in all grades and to raise test scores since the eighties and nineties — less and less room has been left for people to find creative paths toward learning. At the same time, children have spent more and more of their time in school, increasing its impact on their lives.

Chapter Three

The Way Forward

Education Hygiene & Basic Memetic Leadership

I f all this is true and there are reams of research behind it, why are we still using an outdated and potentially harmful model in our education system?

The truth is — and this should come as no surprise to anyone who's ever tried to change a habit or worked in a group of people — that change is hard. The delivery model is deeply embedded in the laws surrounding education, in the logistical apparatus supporting it (the textbooks, testing companies, and administrative support structures), and in the mentality of much of the population, even those who theoretically know better. Every time a politician or parent worries about test scores and every time a parent takes a teacher to task for their kids' grades and the impact that may have on their future, the delivery model is in the background. People rarely confront it directly, but it informs their expectations of the system. Moreover, the negative effects of the delivery model appear slowly, over time, and the connection between the delivery model and its negative effects isn't necessarily obvious to a society in which primary human needs are only vaguely understood.

Returning to miasma theory for a moment, it's important to understand that at the point London diverted its sewage into the Thames, preliminary research had already been done that pointed to the notion of invisible infectious agents leading to disease. This research was dismissed by most, often with prejudice. A particularly dramatic example is that of Dr. Ignaz Semmelweiss. In the early 1840s, by the careful collection and analysis of empirical data, Semmelweiss developed a successful method for reducing the deaths of his patients, mothers who had just given birth. His method? He required the medical students he was teaching, who had just come from the morgue, to wash their hands before attending to maternity patients. This method reduced infections of "puerperal fever" and subsequent deaths by more than 50%. Despite his thoroughly scientific method and the dramatic practical evidence that he was saving lives, he was both professionally and personally ridiculed, and his method was generally rejected until long after his death in 1865.[1]

Letting go of the delivery model is just as difficult for parents and teachers today as letting go of the miasma theory was for physicians over a century ago. Jessica Lahey, a teacher, acknowledges that difficulty when she describes her efforts to explain the seeming paradox of intrinsic motivation to the caring, involved parents of her students. "The less we push our kids toward educational success, the more they will learn," she writes. "The less we use external, or extrinsic, rewards on our children, the more they will engage in their education for the sake and love of learning."[2]

This can feel counterintuitive and frightening. As Alfie Kohn writes in *Punished by Rewards*,[3] "We define ourselves by numbers—take-home pay and cholesterol counts, percentiles (how much does your baby weigh?), and standardized test scores (how much does your child

---

1. Wootton (2007) pp. 215–217.

2. Lahey (2015) p. 22.

3. Kohn (1999) p. 10.

know?). By contrast, we are uneasy with intangibles and...abstractions such as a sense of well-being or an intrinsic motivation to learn." In a sense, we have little experience of grappling with the world in this way; how can we be certain we're doing the right things to help our kids succeed?

At the institutional level, the delivery model has actively suppressed school practices that center the primary human needs for relatedness and autonomy. In one example, education researchers Andy Hargreaves and Michael Fullan describe how in 1996, Grange Secondary School in Northern England had been identified as struggling. But by 2006, the school had made substantially positive reforms by supporting their primary population of at-risk, poor immigrant children by offering more artistic opportunities. In fact, they transformed the entire school into an integrated arts program.

After that change was fully implemented, the children felt pride in their school and the teachers felt that the new curriculum met their students' needs. While among the poorest 1% of the nation, the school was in the top 2% in growth measures of improvement. Grange Secondary went from 15% of students meeting examination standards in 1996 to over 70% passing in 2008.

The reforms were destroyed in May 2008 when policy decisions above the school level arbitrarily changed the measures of what counted as success.[4] The school was closed in 2010 and replaced by an academy, the UK equivalent of a charter school.[5] The destructive decisions made "sense" within the context of the delivery model because policymakers insisted on imposing the same standards of performance across all schools. But the decisions were clearly counterproductive to a school community that had found creative ways to successfully meet the real needs of its students.

In mainstream schools, teachers are required to operate in an environment that systematically thwarts, or at least neglects, children's primary human needs. And it often thwarts their developmental needs as well, as James P. Comer, founder of the Yale School Development Program, has observed.[6] For decades, the Yale School Development Program has been making substantive improvements in K-12 schools in many states by focusing

---

4. Hargreaves, & Fullan (2012) pp. 10–23

5. Hargreaves, & Harris (2015)

6. Comer (2009)

primarily on relationships.[7] When Comer first started out he noticed that their work could be undermined whenever the principal changed, so he vowed to work at a higher level in the system. Later, he saw that the same problems could arise when the superintendent changed, so he worked a level higher. Over the decades, Comer and his colleagues came to recognize that the improved results they helped create could be undermined or destroyed by policies and politicking at the district or higher levels, just like in the UK example noted above. The challenge we face in aiming for sustainable systemic change is to ensure that there are policies for the support of the needs of children and teachers that are more stable than the people who implement those policies.

If we care about equity in education, our first priority should be to make sure that all students have reliable access to primary need-supportive schools (a systems level goal). Our second priority should be meeting the developmental needs of the children, which the Yale School Development Program has for decades demonstrated to be an effective element of reform (a schools level goal).

---

7. Ibid.

Why Personal Convictions Are Not Enough

In the 1800s, most medical practitioners subscribed to miasma theory. The great irony is that, in education today, most teachers are painfully aware of the delivery model's shortcomings. Most teachers, if the model is explicitly described to them, will tell you immediately that of course learning doesn't work that way.

A useful way to think of it is in terms of growing mental maps. People of all ages continually add information to their brain maps, sometimes shifting their perspectives profoundly, sometimes only filling in details, but this can only happen when information is truly integrated, not just cursorily memorized. Note that in this model, the learner is the active agent. This comes as no surprise to teachers, who know perfectly well that it's precisely the self-directed students, the ones who take control of their own education, who not only master the material but inspire the teacher to be better.

But teachers have limited control over their own practice; they're heavily constrained by the policies of the multilayered bureaucracy above them. There is no sustainable way for individual teachers, by themselves, to take on the responsibility for maintaining the well-being of their students. Effective teaching is not a solo performance; it requires an ensemble, a whole orchestra, in fact. Everyone — teachers, school administrators, specialists, school psychologists, district administrators, consultants, secretaries, parents, policy makers, and so on — has to play his or her part. A teacher may be devoted to the idea of maintaining his or her students' well-being, but if his or her own needs are going unsupported, he or she is unlikely to be able to sustain that for long.

Some teachers manage against the odds to carve out primary human need-supportive spaces. But they do this in the face of an abundance of policies and an even greater abundance of implicit assumptions and practices in school systems that actively undermine their needs and the practices that support their students. To put it another way, there is a pervasive hidden curriculum working against our school system supporting the well-being of the students and staff.

Any alternative to the current system, such as the schools described earlier, feels unfamiliar and can be mired in a swamp of misinformation. People imagine that supporting autonomy, for example, means feral students or children left entirely to their own devices. But this is equivalent to saying that a workplace can't support autonomy without letting its employees run wild. Daniel H. Pink argued in his best-selling book *Drive* that this supposition isn't remotely true. In fact, Pink's account of workplaces such as Google and 3M suggests that in primary need-supportive workplaces, workers actively and enthusiastically engage with the most challenging aspects of the business. In their 2020 book *Humanocracy* Gary Hamel and Michele Zanini also make the case that supporting the autonomy of frontline workers is one of several organizational choices that are highly advantageous. Rather than wildness, autonomy-supportive organizations elicit disciplined enthusiasm when they effectively communicate the nature of their business to their workers.

Perhaps the most seductive appeal of the delivery system is that it seems easy to do. The current highly standardized model of education may be ineffective and, in fact, downright harmful, but it's relatively simple to describe and implement. It takes far more time, thought, and effort to engage with people in ways that support their primary human needs, particularly if the concept is unfamiliar. It's also much harder for politicians to put together sweeping, get-results-quick programs that take primary human needs into account.

An Abundance of Hope

At this point, you may be thinking that we're falling down a gravity well and being sucked into a black hole of educational doom. So it may surprise you to know that the opposite is true. Yes, the modern educational system is based on a fundamentally incorrect model, and yes, change is hard. But change is possible, especially where we're genuinely motivated, and few things motivate us more strongly than the well-being of our children. And there are signs of hope all around us when we know where and how to look for it.

In Chapter 2, we focused on two particular schools to discuss the concept of primary human need support in education. But these are the tips of the iceberg. There are hundreds of schools, using a wide variety of methods and approaches, but all incorporating support for primary human needs, sometimes explicitly, but more often instinctively.[8] Within the public education system itself, there are programs and teachers who manage to push back the dominant paradigm and create a small oasis of autonomy, competence, and relatedness. Think of a teacher who inspired you, who made a subject come alive for you, who gave you confidence in your own abilities and worth. Chances are that this teacher was instinctively supporting your primary needs.

There is every reason to believe that most teachers want to do better by their students than they are currently allowed to; they would support their students' primary needs if they were supported to do so. There are nurturing

---

8. One example: the Yale School Development Program (SDP) has been demonstrating for over forty years that supporting the well-being of children within the school environment is a vital part of successful reform efforts, especially for schools that serve a high proportion of students from marginalized populations. The SDP has focused on three things: pervasively building positive relationships throughout school communities (e.g., relatedness), ensuring that the developmental needs of children inform school decision-making, and viewing schools as complex systems rather than just a relatively simple accumulation of individual interactions.

classrooms and schools all around us, showing us different approaches to the educational process. And we're in a fantastic position at this point in history: We can take advantage of a body of research on learning and education that is extensive and well-supported and has stood up through decades of testing.

There is hope all around us.

So how do we move forward?

The Next Steps

Let's take a moment to acknowledge certain things that won't solve our problems. Contrary to much of the political rhetoric around education, there are no silver bullets. We cannot simply be more committed to education, let the free market take care of things, enshrine parental choice, or pour more money into a dysfunctional system and hope that everything will work out. Nor could we simply try to clone a primary need–supportive school that already exists, even if everyone could agree on which school to replicate, which seems unlikely. Like most problems in the real world, solving this one will require work, ingenuity, and intelligence.

But there are two preliminary steps that will both help students right now and also lay the groundwork for further changes.

The first is to start measuring how well schools support primary human needs or, in other words, how well they nurture their students.

Effective and efficient learning relies on well-being. As long as well-being is routinely compromised, then learning is also compromised. Simply measuring support for primary human needs may seem insufficient, but it's a necessary first step. As a society, we are already oriented toward measurements and tend to focus on problems and solutions that can be framed in terms of data. If we care about primary human needs, and copious research tells us that we should, measuring how well they're supported in school environments is a crucial first step to increasing that support.

Note that this is not an all-encompassing educational theory. There are many discussions about education that need to happen, focusing on teacher training, curriculum development, support structures, and a host of other specific facets of the educational system. It's difficult to decide which should be given attention and which should be ignored, and we don't have an easy answer to that.

What I'm suggesting is that primary-need support — as measured by the psychological well-being of the children being served by schools — is a necessary foundation upon which any successful educational model must be built. Arguing over specific techniques or curricula is pointless when a child arrives at school every day distracted by hunger. If children are struggling to have any of their primary human needs met in school, excellent teaching of a great curriculum is irrelevant.

While some tools for measuring school climate exist most are not implemented in ways that are immediately useful to teachers. Most collect data once a year and report results to teachers weeks later. I am working on a prototype that will enable teachers to get useful results within a day or two and see improvements within weeks. It is called the Formative Climate Assessment.

I will also give a quick shout out to The Hope Survey. The Hope Survey[9] has been validated through peer-reviewed scientific research. It is the only climate measure besides Formative Climate Assessment that is based on Self-Determination Theory (SDT). SDT is the most widely respected and empirically supported model of

---

9. EdVisions (n.d.)

human motivation within the field of psychology. (Note: More measures based on SDT need to be commercialized.)

Second, each of us must nurture the children in our own lives and safeguard their engagement, in school and, more importantly, in life. Often we do this instinctively, but we needn't rely on instinct. Psychological research has provided frameworks we can use to help us support primary human needs.

To start with, we can learn to recognize engagement, or the lack thereof. Simply asking children about how engaged they are may or may not be useful; it isn't difficult for children to realize that we'd prefer a particular answer to that question. But engagement can be roughly recognized by the following, although obtaining an accurate assessment will require more than mere observation.

Recognizing Engagement During an Activity[10]

Behavioral Engagement
- On-task attention and concentration

---

10. Reeve (2012), Reeve, Cheon, & Jang (2020)

- High effort

- High task persistence

Agentic Engagement
- Proactive, intentional, and constructive contribution to the flow of the activity (e.g., offering input, making suggestions)

- Enriching the activity, rather than passively receiving it as a given

Emotions
- Presence of task-facilitating emotions (e.g., interest, curiosity, and enthusiasm)

- Absence of task-withdrawing emotions (e.g., distress, anger, frustration, anxiety, and fear)

Cognitions
- Use of sophisticated, deep, and personalized learning strategies (e.g., elaboration)

- Seeking conceptual understanding rather than surface knowledge (mastery versus performance orientation)

- Use of self-regulatory strategies (e.g., planning)

A more poetic expression of noticing engagement is "measuring the light in their eyes." Parents tend to instinctively understand the importance of that light but can feel that the world tells them to disregard it, to worry instead about performance metrics, such as grades and test scores. But that spark of engagement is crucially important, not only to a child's prospects in life, but to his or her well-being. As a parent once advised me, "The success of a school is indicated by the light in the eyes of its students." If the light in your child's eyes begins to dim, investigate what's going on and consider making changes to the school situation. If it goes out, get your child out of that school. Do everything you can to keep the light in your child's eyes shining bright.

There are specific behaviors that can help to support each of the three primary human needs we've been discussing. The best teachers often instinctively adopt many or all of these behaviors. Although the table below is geared toward a teaching environment, any person interacting with children can benefit from keeping the core principles in mind.

I have two ways of labeling these behaviors. The first, Educational Hygiene (EH), refers to the fact that these are behaviors that are not central to the instructional activities that most people associate with schooling, yet are crucially important. This is similar to how personal hygiene in a medical setting is not central to the treatments that most people associate with medicine, yet are crucially important to controlling the spread of disease.

The second is Basic Memetic Leadership (BML), which refers to the fact that these behaviors will help build the interpersonal cohesion that is necessary for an organization to function well. The following presents the most basic forms while more advanced techniques are the topic of Part 4 of my book Schooling for Holistic Equity.

These are crucial techniques for establishing productive patterns of interaction among the members of the organization at all levels from the classroom to the staff room to the board room. When these behaviors are so well established as patterns in the organization that they do not require any conscious reinforcement, then they form a strong foundation for a positive, nurturing hidden curriculum.

Education Hygiene

NOTE: The following three lists of teacher behaviors are presented in order from most to least impact based on research published in respected peer-reviewed journals.

EDUCATION HYGIENE (EH)
a.k.a. BASIC MEMETIC LEADERSHIP (BML)[11]

EH: Supporting Relatedness
BML: Relational Capital Building

DO

- Show unconditional positive regard for the person (not necessarily their behavior)

- Ask about students' progress, welfare, and/or feelings

- Express affection

- Promote cooperation

- Share teacher enthusiasm

- Show understanding of the students' point of view

- Group students with similar interests

---

11. Sources: Ahmadi (2022) (expert consensus on Do's and Don'ts), Hargreaves & Fullan (2012) (BML terminology)

DON'T

- Apply fair punishments[12]

- Provide conditional positive regard

- Be sarcastic

- Provide rewards unfairly

- Yell or use a harsh tone

- Provide punishments unfairly

- Use abusive language

- Ignore students

---

12. The evidence shows that punishment has negative effects, regardless of whether it is done fairly or not. The experts acknowledge that punishment might be necessary under some circumstances. If it becomes necessary, then it should be done fairly in order to minimize the motivational damage it will do.

EH: Supporting Autonomy
BML: Decisional Capital Building

DO

- Allow for student input or choice

- Teach in students' preferred ways

- Provide rationales [for requirements]

- Allow student self-paced progress

- Rely on invitational language

- Ask students about their experience of lessons

- Teach students to set intrinsic life goals for learning

- Provide a variety of activities

- Provoke curiosity

- Discuss class values

- Provide extra resources for independent learning

DON'T

- Exhibit solutions or answers

- Use praise as a contingent reward

- Set pressuring deadlines

- Set up activities that exclude some students

- Use pressuring language

EH: Supporting Competence
BML: Human Capital Building

DO

- Provide optimal challenge

- Provide specific feedback

- Praise improvement or effort

- Provide feedback aimed at improvement or effort

- Praise specific action

- Use praise fairly

- Set goals based on self-referenced standards

- Display hope, encouragement, and optimism

- Demonstrate examples

- Provide feedback in private

- Clarify expectations

- Display explicit guidance

- Ask questions to expand understanding

- Facilitate self-monitoring of progress and effort

- Encourage active learning

- Offer hints

- Use pupils as positive role models

DON'T
- Group students on the basis of ability

- Set goals where students compete against each other

- Praise winning via peer comparison

- Use vague criticism

- Give undifferentiated challenges

- Offer chaotic or absentee teaching

- Criticize losing via peer comparison

- Criticize a fixed quality

- Publicly present critical feedback

There is an implicit assumption in American society that nurturing is somehow antithetical to being professional. The detailed arguments for education hygiene and memetic leadership are presented in my book Schooling for Holistic Equity, but my labels for them can be used by professionals when they want to refer to these nurturing behaviors without implicitly diminishing their professionalism. I wrote Schooling for Holistic Equity to build a coherent and far-reaching case against this assumption. If we assign "professionals" to solve a human problem and then undermine their ability to support the primary human needs of suffering humans, from the perspective of psychology, we have blindfolded them, tied their hands behind their backs, and stabbed them as well.

In order to root out this pernicious assumption, it is necessary to fully reimagine our ideas about education.

Up to this point, the focus of the book has primarily been on the dilemma that parents face. In the final chapter of this second edition I, Don, will present a couple of key points to outline the dilemma that is faced by teachers and all the other professionals who serve in K-12 schools.

Chapter Four

Towards An Integrated Perspective

D ilemmas are situations in which the available choices of action create a conflict between two or more values. The best possible resolution of any dilemma is to eliminate the conflict, though that is a rare outcome. The more common course of action is to simply choose one of the courses of action and, if possible, mitigate the downsides of sacrificing one value at the expense of another.

Global education systems have been operating for decades (perhaps centuries) in a manner that has actively sacrificed some values at the expense of others. There have been fights that have, at times, denied the validity of some values. In particular, the Back-to-Basics movement in its simplest incarnation from the late 60s and early 70s promoted a simple, politically expedient model that denied the value of having schools provide services beyond delivery of the 3Rs of academics. Different values may have been sacrificed at different times. Globally school systems may have made a variety of sacrifices, but it is clear from the global extent of the challenges in schooling that there are sacrifices being made almost everywhere. It also seems likely to me that some (perhaps most) of those sacrifices may have been made in ignorance of what the downside costs were going to be.

It is no longer morally valid to posit the continuation of such sacrifices when a means of resolving the conflict has become possible. I believe that such a resolution is now possible in the context of schooling due to the development of Self-Determination Theory (SDT). SDT is the most thoroughly supported scientific theory of motivation and engagement. But before I explain how that resolution can work, let's take a look at some examples of how we arrive at certain types of truth.

Back in 1872, a poet named John Godfrey Saxe wrote a famous poem that portrays one of the key challenges we face. Note that he assumed a perspective that must be given a carefully nuanced interpretation in light of what we know about the limitations of knowledge and the human mind, which I will discuss afterward. The poem was originally titled, "The Blind Men and the Elephant: A Hindoo Fable," although the story was also found in the Buddhist, Sufi, and Jain traditions.

The Blind Men And The Elephant

It was six men of Indosta
To learning much inclined,
Who went to see the Elephant
(Though all of them were blind),
That each by observation
Might satisfy his mind.

The First approached the Elephant,
And happening to fall
Against his broad and sturdy side,
At once began to bawl:
"God bless me!—but the Elephant
Is very like a wall!"

The Second, feeling of the tusk,
Cried: "Ho!—what have we here

So very round and smooth and sharp?
To me 'tis mighty clear
This wonder of an Elephant
Is very like a spear!"

The Third approached the animal,
And happening to take
The squirming trunk within his hands,
Thus boldly up and spake:
"I see," quoth he, "the Elephant
Is very like a snake!"

The Fourth reached out his eager hand,
And felt about the knee.
"What most this wondrous beast is like
Is mighty plain," quoth he;
"'Tis clear enough the Elephant
Is very like a tree!"

The Fifth, who chanced to touch the ear,
Said: "E'en the blindest man
Can tell what this resembles most;
Deny the fact who can,
This marvel of an Elephant
Is very like a fan!"

The Sixth no sooner had begun
About the beast to grope,
Than, seizing on the swinging tail
That fell within his scope,
"I see," quoth he, "the Elephant
Is very like a rope!"

And so these men of Indostan
Disputed loud and long,
Each in his own opinion
Exceeding stiff and strong,
Though each was partly in the right,
And all were in the wrong!

So, oft in theologic wars
The disputants, I ween,
Rail on in utter ignorance
Of what each other mean,
And prate about an Elephant
Not one of them has seen!

This poem is an observation that "theologic wars" are about things that none of the warring parties can see. The story presumes that seeing the thing at issue could resolve conflicts about it. Compelling though it is, notice that the issue of the nature of the elephant is only "resolved" for us by the assumption that the entire essence of being an elephant is available to be seen. That resolution presumes we know the essence of the elephant by sight alone. That is obviously not the case, but we feel superior to the blind men despite the fact that most of us know little more than they do about the true nature of an elephant. The poem does not communicate how blind we all are and how we will forever remain blind to the true nature of reality. (If you would like a more thorough justification of this claim you can read *Schooling For Holistic Equity*.)

It is fitting that this poem has its origin in religion and is often also applied to science. Both are equally valiant attempts to understand reality. It applies to many other fields of human endeavor, as well. Every religion has had at one time or another the humility to admit that it is ignorant of the true nature of reality. Prophets of every religious persuasion have stated that God is unknowable. Religious scholar Reverend Michael Dowd suggests that equating the term "God" with the term "reality" helps us to better understand what we're dealing with in both religion and science. Problems only arise from taking metaphors to be literally true.

We can look at the term "God" in a less literal way. Take zero as a parallel example. Zero is an absential character of certain numbers, a numerical placeholder. Zero did not exist in the Greek numerical system, so it was fiendishly difficult to do many types of computations. It turned out that having a placeholder for an absence of value was really helpful in mathematics.

I understand the word God as a placeholder that indicates an absence of knowledge. So I believe in God in the same way that I believe in zero. Whenever I use either term, I am indicating an absence. I am admitting that I am blind to reality and acknowledging that it has causal powers over me that I don't understand.

Science is also blind to reality. While science can explain many things in principle due to the amazing reliability of the central dogmas of physics, chemistry, and biology, explanations are not the same thing as knowing in practice. No scientist can precisely answer the question of how many elephants are pooping right now. There is a clear and specific whole number answer to that question, but we cannot know it except in imprecise probabilistic terms. There are infinitely many questions that have answers that are available only in principle or in vague probabilistic ways.

Science works by focusing in on thin slices of our reality-hiding interface. Science has collectively learned more and more about how our reality-hiding interface seems to work. Revealing the fact that we operate within an interface rather than directly within reality is a triumph of science, even if many, perhaps most, scientists themselves are not comfortable with this revelation. We have a few central dogmas in the sciences that have been translated into practical applications that have generated miraculous technologies for our society. But beyond those central dogmas, we are woefully ignorant and blind to the true nature of reality. Scientists and religious scholars are equally blind to reality, though the scientists have done a better job working out causal models that give us all everyday miracles like lightbulbs and iPhones.

We need to recognize that the central core of educational equity is needs and that our needs are hidden from us. This is not surprising, but we need to practice humility in our quest to achieve equity. We would do well to view ourselves, in ultimate terms, as being just as blind as everyone else. I am confident that both the principles and practical applications that I am sharing are well validated by many prior scientists upon whose shoulders I am standing. I suggest we work together to figure out how to proceed using the latest scientific insights.

Reality is Hidden

The hiddenness of reality is accepted as true across many disciplines besides religion. It is certainly true of science, which is the context in which I first heard the elephant parable.

Physicists since ancient times had been debating the nature of light. Is light a wave or a particle? The use of an either/or construction for the question invoked the logic of mutual exclusivity. That mutual exclusivity cognitively framed what the scientists thought could be true. A logical move, but ultimately incorrect. The reality of light turned out to be a "both/and" proposition. Turns out that it is both; light is waves and particles, or wavicles.

Biologists finally resolved the "nature versus nurture" debate recently. The question was what causes animal behavior? Is it the genes inherited from an individual's parents? Or is it the environment encountered throughout life? Charles Darwin's cousin, Francis Galton, was the one who framed the debate by coining the phrase "nature versus nurture." The actual question took around a hundred years to resolve. The recent discovery of epigenetics showed us once again that our insistence on describing reality using mutually exclusive categories was dead wrong. It is both nature and nurture.

It might be helpful to think of these as issues about what belongs in which categories. Does light fit into the wave category or the particle category? Does biological inheritance fit into the genetics (nature) category or the experience (nurture) category? The truth has been revealed to be that each of those mutually exclusive formulations was the incorrect proposition, it was a better description of reality to posit the categories as working in concert with each other rather than being mutually exclusive. The truth resides at the intersections.

In education, I believe that we have a slightly different problem. Rather than the mutual exclusivity of only two options we face the problem of having to resolve dilemmas created by the existence of three, five, and six relevant categories. What we have now in the dominant mainstreams of education around the world are instances of what I will call the exclusion delusion. Each system has picked one or more categories to draw upon for their operating principles, but they have also tended, for the sake of simplicity and political expedience, to exclude the consideration of any other principles. The exclusion produces a form of blindness to the values, and therefore the human psychological sacrifices, that are embodied by those competing conceptions.

The dilemmas of education can be resolved by regarding the inclusive pattern to hold true in three specific areas: learning, teaching, and schooling.

Drawing on research by John Hattie and his colleague Nola Purdie it turns out that there are a limited number of conceptions about learning in the world.

The conceptions are: gaining information; personal change; remembering, understanding, and using information; development of social competence; and that learning is unbound by time & space. Those first five were found in Western societies, but when they made their inquiries in Eastern societies they found that they had to add a sixth item: the duty to learn.

The Exclusion Delusion

So the point I want to make here is that we have policies in schools and in public policy more broadly that may be assuming that only some of these are valid. If the only thing that public policy accepts as valid learning is dutifully gaining, remembering, understanding, and using information then that is a symptom of the exclusion delusion.

The exclusion delusion in this instance is going to result in shallower learning. When we take the whole phenomena of learning seriously we will get the deeper learning that is necessary in today's world.

Moving on to teaching I am drawing on the work of a researcher named Daniel Pratt and his associates who cataloged conceptions of teaching and arrived at five different ways of understanding it. Those ways of conceiving of teaching are: delivery, nurturing, transformation, immersion, and social influence. The typical exclusion delusion for teaching is that the teacher's job is limited to the nurturing delivery of knowledge, skills, and information.

Many folks dream of a little schoolhouse on the prairie in which a maidenly school marm hired by the local townsfolk delivers the 3Rs with a stick in one hand and a piece of chalk in the other. When those kinds of delusionally oversimplified conceptions of teaching are backed by political power, then we get the disastrous results in schools that I mentioned previously.

Remember, there is some degree of truth underlying these conceptions, but it creates disastrous results when political forces impose these conceptions to the exclusion of other valid ways of thinking about how to educate children. This is similar to how the notion that bad smells cause disease is partly right because there are toxic gasses, airborne germs, and the presence of carrion, raw sewage, and other noxious stenches do have some correlation with some diseases. Delivery is wrong as the exclusive source of organizational principles for managing schools that educate children. If it is put in its proper place as one of many sources of those principles, then we're good.

The question here is, What do we get when all of the conceptions of teaching are honored? I suggest that we will get what I call a Catalytic Pedagogy, which I present in my book *Schooling for Holistic Equity*. If you want more details immediately I encourage you to watch the video on the home page at HolisticEquity.org.

Now we turn to schooling. I have observed that there are schools across a spectrum from mainstream to radically different from that mainstream. I have been to education conferences all around the world put on by organizations that operate in every way imaginable. The most mainstream conference was the ASCD conference, the most radical being the International Democratic Education Conference which in 2022 was doubling as the Summerhill Festival of Childhood. There are three categories that I see as the most distinctive.

The first is the category of Accountability, which is the most prominent feature of the mainstream. Second, there is a significant movement to incorporate Social Justice into schools. The final category comes from how stridently the folks in the democratic education movement are championing Freedom.

The psychologist Peter Gray who has a blog on Psychology Today has written quite a bit about how important freedom is and how incompatible he believes the mainstream to be with that view. He did some formal studies of Sudbury Valley School, which is one of the most well-known democratic schools, and also where he sent his son. The exclusion delusion is particularly strong in this case because there is a pattern of the mainstream steadily eroding and eventually destroying schools that wear the mantle of Freedom when they are beholden to public funding sources. Thus, the folks on this educational freedom train are reluctant to seek out that type of funding and their schooling options are usually relegated to those who can afford it.

The apparent mutual exclusivity is an accurate and true observation, but that does not warrant the conclusion that the mutual exclusivity is necessary. I propose that if we can identify the core truth behind each of these three perspectives, then we can arrive at a logical means of rectifying the discrepancies to arrive at a consilient view that gives us all a path towards meaningful reform. The core truths that I see in the schools are drawn from the primary psychological needs that all human beings have and that have been shown to be central to the deeper learning that we expect schools to facilitate.

The mainstream Accountability view is anchored in the truth that all humans have the need to be competent; to perceive themselves as effective agents who pursue goals that are meaningful to both themselves and their community. Unfortunately, that truth becomes distorted by the systems of academic bookkeeping that are used as stand-ins for actual learning. The system cannot tell the difference between someone who faked their way through getting grades, test scores, certificates, and diplomas and someone who was genuinely intrigued by their studies and mastered the subjects they were taught.

The Social Justice view is based on the universal human need for relatedness, the perception that you belong to a group and are accepted for who you are within that group. The many ways that isolation and fragmentation occur in our society have a disproportionate effect on those who are marginalized, thus the typical social justice focus is on those groups. But even beyond that, the negative effects harm the majority, too. Gallup data shows that the global workforce is disengaged at rates ranging from 70-85% depending on the country. That is an indication of pervasive psychological harms being done. The harms are spread across all populations, though it is true that the marginalized are harmed disproportionately.

The Freedom view makes the primary need for autonomy a central consideration. Everyone needs to perceive themselves as the cause of their own activities and to express their will in the world. Unfortunately, schools that honor this need are extremely few and far between, and as I mentioned before they tend to get weeded out of publicly funded systems. There are numerous models of innovation that say they are doing better at incorporating autonomy into their programs, but they don't have solid evidence to support the claim. As I mentioned before I am developing a prototype assessment system to help address this deficiency. It is called the Formative Climate Assessment.

So what is at the center where all three of these categories overlap? All the major pieces of my work land in the intersection. The branded version is Attitutor Schooling. Catalytic pedagogy, which I mentioned earlier, is a more generic phrase for it. A pedagogy is catalytic when it has evidence that shows that both teachers and students are more internally rather than externally motivated, have their primary psychological needs met, and are engaged more agentically, not just behaviorally.

My strategic plan for helping schools to become Attitutor Schools is called Back-to-Basics 2.0. And the intended outcome of all that other stuff is Holistic Equity. I use the term "holistic" to ensure that we are talking about meeting the needs of all the humans in the system, not just some of them. My book *Schooling for Holistic Equity* is where I have gathered together the most comprehensive argument for this type of consilient view of education that can lay the groundwork for countering the exclusion delusion.

Changing the System

The system I am concerned with is K-12, the part of education that is meant to serve children. In order to affect meaningful change it is necessary to characterize the system and then change one of the characteristics of the system. In the simplest terms possible the school system today is dependent on data. If we can change the character of the data the system is dependent upon, then we will change the character of the system. Currently, the system is focused almost exclusively on academic data. There has been an opening under ESSA to introduce non-academic data streams, so that is an opening we can take advantage of. From that perspective what I am proposing is to introduce a better climate measure.

From the perspective of catalytic pedagogy, I am proposing that we measure and manage the experiences that students and teachers have in their schools. The top priority is to find out how well teachers' efforts to support the primary psychological needs of their students are succeeding. The Formative Climate Assessment starts off with measures of the provisions that teachers are using to support students mixed in with how well the students' needs are being satisfied. Eventually, motivation and engagement measures will also be included to provide a more complete picture.

As I am developing the prototype I am also figuring out how to get this tool into the hands of as many teachers as possible. Every established climate measure that I am aware of collects data only once or twice a year, focuses their analysis on painting a broad high-level picture of the climate, and are not capable of getting the information back to teachers within a day or two. The Formative Climate Assessment is designed to be used many times a year, analysis is focused on specific classroom- and teacher-level experiences, and enables teachers to get useful information within a day or two. Those other measures will work in tandem with ours by providing third-party validation of what teachers will be accomplishing with the Formative Climate Assessment. The ideal situation in my mind today is a network of teachers mutually supporting each other to use the Formative Climate Assessment effectively backed up by a small team of technical folks who ensure that the minimal technology needed to use it functions as easily and seamlessly as possible.

In conclusion, I just want to say that just because most schools don't fit today does not mean that they will continue not to fit in the future. We can and should integrate the competing perspectives on learning, teaching, and schooling in order to better grasp the reality of education. That is a truth that will set us free.

References

Ahmadi, A., Noetel, M., Parker, P. D., Ryan, R., Ntoumanis, N., Reeve, J., ... Lonsdale, C. (2022, February 4). *A Classification System for Teachers' Motivational Behaviors Recommended in Self-Determination Theory Interventions.*

Berg, D. (2022). *Schooling for Holistic Equity: How to manage the hidden curriculum in K-12.* New Haven, CT: Publish Your Purpose.

Berg, D. A., & Corpus, J. H. (2013). "Enthusiastic Students: A Study Of Motivation In Two Alternatives To Mandatory Instruction. *Other Education, 2*(2), 42–66.

Berr, J. (2016). Employers: New College Grads Aren't Ready for Workplace. *CBS News Money Watch.* Retrieved from

Bouffard, T., Marcoux, M., Vezeau, C., & Bordeleau, L. (2003). "Changes in Self-Perceptions of Competence and Intrinsic Motivation Among Elementary School Children." *British Journal of Educational Psychology, 73,* 171-186.

Comer, J. P. (2009). *What I Learned in School: Reflections on Race, Child Development, and School Reform.* San Francisco: Jossey-Bass.

Corpus, J. H., Mcclintic-Gilbert, M. S., & Hayenga, A. O. (2009). "Within-Year Changes in Children's Intrinsic and Extrinsic Motivational Orientations: Contextual Predictors and Academic Outcomes." *Contemporary Educational Psychology, 34*(2), 154–166. doi:10.1016/j.cedpsych.2009.01.001

EdVisions. (n.d.). "Student Motivation." Retrieved June 14, 2017, from

Gardner, H. (2004). *The Unschooled Mind: How Children Think and How Schools Should Teach.* New York, NY: Basic Books.

Gottfried, A. E., Fleming, J. S., & Gottfried, A. W. (2001). "Continuity of Academic Intrinsic Motivation from Childhood through Late Adolescence: A Longitudinal Study." *Journal of Educational Psychology, 93*(1), 3–13. doi:10.1037//0022-0663.93.1.3

Gray, P. (2013). *Free to Learn: Why Unleashing the Instinct to Play Will Make Our Children Happier, More*

Self-Reliant, and Better Students for Life. New York, NY: Basic Books.

Haas, E., Fischman, G., & Brewer, J. (2014). *Dumb Ideas Won't Create Smart Kids: Straight Talk about Bad School Reform, Good Teaching, and Better Learning*. New York and London: Teachers College Press.

Hargreaves, A., & Fullan, M. (2012). *Professional Capital: Transforming Teaching in Every School*. New York, NY: Teachers College Press.

Hargreaves, A., & Harris, A. (2015). "High Performance Leadership in Unusually Challenging Educational Circumstances." Eesti Haridusteaduste Ajakiri. *Estonian Journal of Education, 3(1)*, 28. DOI: 10.12697/eha.2015.3.1.02b

Harter, S. (1981). "A New Self-Report Scale of Intrinsic Versus Extrinsic Orientation in the Classroom: Motivational and Informational Components." *Developmental Psychology, 17*(3), 300–312. doi:10.1037//0012-1649.17.3.300

Hunter, J.P., & Csikszentmihalyi, M. (2003). "The Positive Psychology of Interested Adolescents." *Journal of Youth and Adolescence, 32*(1) 27-35. DOI: 10.1023/A:1021028306392

Johnson, S. (2006). *The Ghost Map: The Story of London's Most Terrifying Epidemic--and How it Changed*

Science, Cities, and the Modern World. New York: Riverhead Books.

Kohn, Alfie. (1999). *Punished by Rewards.* New York: Houghton Mifflin Company.

Lahey, Jessica. (2015). *The Gift of Failure.* New York: HarperCollins.

Lepper, M. R., Corpus, J. H., & Iyengar, S. S. (2005). "Intrinsic and Extrinsic Motivational Orientations in the Classroom: Age Differences and Academic Correlates." *Journal of Educational Psychology, 97*(2), 184–196. doi:10.1037/0022-0663.97.2.184

NCES (National Center for Education Statistics). (2016). "Fast Facts: Dropout rate." National Center for Education Statistics (NCES), a part of the U.S. Department of Education. Retrieved May 18, 2017, from

Nord, C., Roey, S., Perkins, R., Lyons, M., Lemanski, N., Brown, J., & Schuknecht, J. (2011). *The Nation's Report Card: America's High School Graduates* (NCES 2011-462). U.S. Department of Education, National Center for Education Statistics. Washington, DC: U.S. Government Printing Office.

Pink, D. H. (2011). *Drive.* Penguin Group US.

Pratt, D. D., Arseneau, R., Boldt, A., Johnson, J., Nesbit, T., Rodenburg, D., & T'Kenye, C. (2005). *Five*

Perspectives on Teaching in Adult and Higher Education. Krieger Publishing Company.

Purdie, N., & Hattie, J. (2002). Assessing Students' Conceptions of Learning. *Australian Journal of Educational and Developmental Psychology*, 2, 17–32.

Reeve, J. (2012). "A Self-Determination Theory Perspective on Student Engagement." In S. L. Christenson et al. (eds.), *Handbook of Research on Student Engagement.* New York: Springer. DOI: 10.1007/978-1-4614-2018-7_7 pp. 149–172

Reeve, J., Cheon, S.H., Jang, H. (2020) "How and Why Students Make Academic Progress: Reconceptualizing the Student Engagement Construct to Increase its Explanatory Power." *Contemporary Educational Psychology 62.*

U.S. Department of Education. (2005). "10 Facts about K-12 Education Funding." Washington, DC: Author. Retrieved from

Wootton, D. (2007). *Bad Medicine.* New York, NY: Oxford University Press.

Zhao, Y. (2009). "Catching Up, or, Leading the Way: American Education in the Age of Globalization." Alexandria, VA: Association for Supervision and Curriculum Development.

Also By Don Berg

Attitude First

Every Parent's Dilemma

Education Can Only Be Offered

More Joy More Genius

Unfailing Schools

Schooling for Holistic Equity

The $6 Billion Reading First Failure:
The Difference Made By A Definition

Made in the USA
Middletown, DE
28 April 2023